jump

Grammar
and Spelling

5

Nick Beare
Jeanette Greenwell

MACMILLAN

Macmillan

Companies and representatives throughout the world

Jump 5

Text D.R. © Nick Beare, Jeanette Greenwell 2002
Design and illustrations D.R. © Macmillan Publishers S.A. de C.V. 2002

First edition 2002
Reprinted 2003, 2005, 2006 (twice), 2007 (twice), 2008 (twice), 2010

Design: Macmillan Publishers S.A. de C.V.
Page make-up: Bosquejo Arte y Diseño
Cover design: Gilberto Bobadilla
Cover artwork: Jésica Segundo
Illustrations: Gilberto Bobadilla, Jésica Segundo

CANIEM No. 2275

ISBN: 978-970-650-132-5

Macmillan Publishers S.A. de C.V.
Insurgentes Sur 1886
Col. Florida
Delegación Álvaro Obregón
C.P. 01030 México, D.F.
Tel: (55) 5482 2200
elt@grupomacmillan.com
A wholly owned subsidiary of Macmillan Publishers Holdings Ltd

www.macmillan.com.mx
www.macmillanenglish.com
www.grupomacmillan.com

Impreso en México

Esta obra se terminó de imprimir
en julio de 2010 en los talleres de
Impresos Santiago, S.A. de C.V.,
con domicilio en: Trigo No. 80,
Col. Granjas Esmeralda
Del. Iztapalapa, México, D.F.

2013   2012   2011   2010   2009
19   18   17   16   15   14   13   12   11   10

Contents

Unit 1				
	Lesson 1	Review	Present simple and past simple	6
	Lesson 2	Review	Future with *going to*	7
	Lesson 3	Review	Review – all tenses	8
	Lesson 4	Review	Past progressive	9
	Lesson 5	Review	Comparative adjectives	10
	Lesson 6	Review	Superlative adjectives	11
	Lesson 7	Review	Present perfect	12
	Lesson 8	Review	*have to* and *will*	13
	Lesson 9	Review	*can* and *can't*	14
	Lesson 10	Fun Page	Adventures with Eric Explorer: At the market	15
	Review 1	Evaluation	Grammar Review	16
	Review 2	Evaluation	Grammar Review	17

Unit 2				
	Lesson 1	Practice	Present perfect/Affirmative and negative	18
	Lesson 2	Practice	Present perfect questions	19
	Lesson 3	Practice	Past simple and present perfect	20
	Lesson 4	Grammar	Has she ever…? Have you ever…?	21
	Lesson 5	Grammar	I've never…	22
	Lesson 6	Grammar	I like swimming.	23
	Lesson 7	Grammar	I'm good at cooking.	24
	Lesson 8	Grammar	Cooking is fun.	25
	Lesson 9	Spelling	Spelling words with *ee* and *ea*	26
	Lesson 10	Fun Page	Adventures with Eric Explorer: In the Arctic	27
	Review 1	Evaluation	Grammar Review	28
	Review 2	Evaluation	Grammar Review	29

Unit 3				
	Lesson 1	Grammar	If he goes to the Amazon…	30
	Lesson 2	Practice	First conditional	31
	Lesson 3	Practice	If she paints her bedroom…	32
	Lesson 4	Practice	If I don't study…	33
	Lesson 5	Grammar	*may/might* or *going to*	34
	Lesson 6	Practice	He may/might go out.	35
	Lesson 7	Grammar	He could jump into the river.	36
	Lesson 8	Practice	First conditional with *may/might*	37
	Lesson 9	Spelling	Spelling words with silent letters	38
	Lesson 10	Fun Page	Adventures with Eric Explorer: A puzzle for Eric	39
	Review 1	Evaluation	Grammar Review	40
	Review 2	Evaluation	Grammar Review	41

Unit 4				
	Lesson 1	Grammar	The potatoes are washed.	42
	Lesson 2	Practice	Present simple passive	43
	Lesson 3	Grammar	Present simple passive with *by*	44
	Lesson 4	Grammar	Present simple passive/Questions and negatives	45

Contents

	Lesson 5	Vocabulary	A school play	46
	Lesson 6	Grammar	The program was designed by the students.	47
	Lesson 7	Practice	It wasn't won by…	48
	Lesson 8	Grammar	Who was it written by?	49
	Lesson 9	Spelling	Spelling words with *oo*	50
	Lesson 10	Fun Page	Adventures with Eric Explorer: Tom Lott's treasure	51
	Review 1	Evaluation	Grammar Review	52
	Review 2	Evaluation	Grammar Review	53
Unit 5	Lesson 1	Practice	Making questions	54
	Lesson 2	Practice	Making questions	55
	Lesson 3	Practice	Question words	56
	Lesson 4	Vocabulary	On vacation	57
	Lesson 5	Grammar	Questions with *Who…?*	58
	Lesson 6	Practice	Questions with *Who…?*	59
	Lesson 7	Grammar	Connectors	60
	Lesson 8	Practice	Punctuation	61
	Lesson 9	Spelling	Spelling words with *ou* or *ow*	62
	Lesson 10	Fun Page	Adventures with Eric Explorer: The mystery package	63
	Review 1	Evaluation	Grammar Review	64
	Review 2	Evaluation	Grammar Review	65
Unit 6	Lesson 1	Vocabulary	Prepositions	66
	Lesson 2	Vocabulary	Prepositions	67
	Lesson 3	Practice	Following directions	68
	Lesson 4	Practice	Giving directions	69
	Lesson 5	Grammar	Reporting orders	70
	Lesson 6	Grammar	He told him to…/He told him not to…	71
	Lesson 7	Practice	He asked her to…/He asked her not to…	72
	Lesson 8	Practice	Reported orders and polite requests	73
	Lesson 9	Spelling	Spelling words with vowel + *r*	74
	Lesson 10	Fun Page	Adventures with Eric Explorer: A meeting downtown	75
	Review 1	Evaluation	Grammar Review	76
	Review 2	Evaluation	Grammar Review	77
Unit 7	Lesson 1	Grammar	Quotation marks	78
	Lesson 2	Practice	Quotation marks	79
	Lesson 3	Grammar	She said…	80
	Lesson 4	Practice	Reported statements	81
	Lesson 5	Practice	He said that…	82
	Lesson 6	Practice	He said he was an explorer.	83
	Lesson 7	Practice	They said…	84
	Lesson 8	Practice	He said that he liked his cats.	85

Contents

	Lesson 9	Spelling	Spelling words with vowel combinations	86
	Lesson 10	Fun Page	Adventures with Eric Explorer: The mysterious clues	87
	Review 1	Evaluation	Grammar Review	88
	Review 2	Evaluation	Grammar Review	89
Unit 8	Lesson 1	Vocabulary	Occupations	90
	Lesson 2	Grammar	I asked her if…	91
	Lesson 3	Practice	We asked her if…	92
	Lesson 4	Practice	He asked me if…	93
	Lesson 5	Practice	Reported questions with *if*…	94
	Lesson 6	Grammar	Reported *Wh-* questions	95
	Lesson 7	Practice	He asked me why…	96
	Lesson 8	Practice	Reported questions	97
	Lesson 9	Spelling	Spelling words with *s* + consonant	98
	Lesson 10	Fun Page	Adventures with Eric Explorer: Favorite things	99
	Review 1	Evaluation	Grammar Review	100
	Review 2	Evaluation	Grammar Review	101
Unit 9	Lesson 1	Grammar	He had cleaned his bedroom.	102
	Lesson 2	Practice	He hadn't cleaned his bedroom.	103
	Lesson 3	Grammar	Past perfect with *already*	104
	Lesson 4	Practice	Past perfect with *already*	105
	Lesson 5	Grammar	Past perfect with *never* and *before*	106
	Lesson 6	Grammar	You should study in the evening.	107
	Lesson 7	Practice	*should* and *shouldn't*	108
	Lesson 8	Practice	*should* and *shouldn't*	109
	Lesson 9	Spelling	Spelling letters with the same sound	110
	Lesson 10	Fun Page	Adventures with Eric Explorer: The puzzle on the wall	111
	Review 1	Evaluation	Grammar Review	112
	Review 2	Evaluation	Grammar Review	113
Unit 10	Lesson 1	Grammar	a lot of/lots/a few/a little	114
	Lesson 2	Practice	How much…? How many…?	115
	Lesson 3	Practice	Quantifiers	116
	Lesson 4	Grammar	It was so hot that…	117
	Lesson 5	Practice	Verb table	118
	Lesson 6	Practice	Verb table	119
	Lesson 7	Practice	Which tense?	120
	Lesson 8	Practice	Which tense?	121
	Lesson 9	Spelling	Spelling words that end with *–tion*	122
	Lesson 10	Fun Page	Adventures with Eric Explorer: Eric is writing a book.	123
	Review 1	Evaluation	Grammar Review	124
	Review 2	Evaluation	Grammar Review	125

Unit 1
Lesson 1

Present simple and past simple

1 Complete the questions and answer them.

All about me

1. _____Whats_____ your name?

   My name is _____.

2. Where _____ you live?

   _____.

3. Where do you _____ to school?

   _____.

4. How many brothers and sisters do you _____?

   _____.

5. What time _____ get up?

   _____.

6. What time do _____ to bed?

   _____.

7. _____ you like hamburgers?

   _____.

2 Write about two things you did and didn't do last week.

1. _____.

2. _____.

3. _____.

4. _____.

Review

Lesson 2

Future with *going to*

1 **Write about two things you're going to do and two things you aren't going to do this evening.**

1 _____.

2 _____.

3 _____.

4 _____.

2 **Answer the questions.**

1 Are you going to go on a trip next weekend?

_____.

2 Are you going to play sport next week?

_____.

3 What are you going to do next Friday?

_____.

4 When are you going to have an exam?

_____.

3 **Write a paragraph about your plans for the future.**

I'm going to _____

_____

_____

_____

_____

Review

1 Write questions about Eric.

1   ___What's his_____ name?
Eric Explorer.

2   _____ live?
In Canada.

3   _____ now?
He's talking to Annie Intrepid.

4   _____ last week?
He explored the Amazon.

5   _____ next week?
He's going to fly to the Antarctic.

2 Ask Eric questions about Annie. Write his answers.

ANNIE INTREPID

AGE: 21
ADDRESS: 17 Flower Street, Toronto, Canada
TELEPHONE: 235-7831

You: ___How old is Annie_____?
Eric: _____.
You: _____?
Eric: _____.
You: _____?
Eric: _____.

Lesson 4

Past progressive

At Mrs. Mystery's house yesterday…

Mr. Black

Mrs. Mystery

1 Complete the sentences.

Mr. Black (talk) ___was talking___ on the phone.

Mrs. Mystery (not, talk) _____ on the phone.

She (listen) _____ to music. The cats (drink, milk)

_____. The crocodiles (not, drink, milk) _____

_____. They (sleep) _____.

2 Complete the questions and answers.

(1) ___What was___ Mrs. Mystery ___doing___?

She was listening to music.

(2) _____ Mr. Black _____?

_____.

(3) _____ the crocodiles _____?

Yes, they _____.

(4) _____ the cats _____?

No, they _____.

(5) _____ Mrs. Mystery _____ to music?

_____.

Review

Comparative adjectives

1 Write the names of two cities in your country.

_____ and _____

Complete the sentences about the cities.

(1) _____ is smaller than _____ .

(2) _____ is bigger than _____ .

(3) _____ is more attractive than _____ .

(4) _____ isn't as attractive as _____ .

2 Write a paragraph comparing the cities.
Use these adjectives:

polluted   clean   safe   busy   quiet

Review

Lesson 6

Superlative adjectives

1 Complete the sentences with your opinions.

I think…

1 the best actor is _____.

2 the funniest television program is _____.

3 the most boring television program is _____.

4 the easiest school subject is _____.

5 the most difficult school subject is _____.

2 Write sentences about the people in your class. Use these adjectives:

| young | old | intelligent | funny | friendly | tall |

Example: *Victoria is the funniest person in the class.*

1 _____.

2 _____.

3 _____.

4 _____.

5 _____.

6 _____.

Review

Present perfect

Write an affirmative and a negative sentence for each topic.

Books

1   I've read The Little Prince _____.

2   I haven't read Don Quijote _____.

Movies

3   _____.

4   _____.

Places

5   _____.

6   _____.

Food

7   _____.

8   _____.

Drink

9   _____.

10   _____.

Television programs

11   _____.

12   _____.

Music

13   _____.

14   _____.

Review

Lesson 8

have to **and** will

1 Complete the sentences about your school with these words:

> have to   don't have to   has to   doesn't have to

1 I _____ arrive at school on time.

2 I _____ go to school on Saturday.

3 I _____ do homework in the evening.

4 The teacher _____ grade our exams.

5 The teacher _____ wear a hat.

6 We _____ pay attention to the teacher.

7 We _____ sweep the classroom floor.

2 Write three more sentences about people's obligations at your school.

1 I _____.

2 The teacher _____.

3 We _____.

3 Make predictions with will **and** won't.

When I'm 21…

1 I _____.

2 I _____.

3 my friends _____.

4 my family _____.

Review

can and can't

1 Put the words in the correct order. Answer the questions.

(1) / you / a car / drive / Can /

_____? _____.

(2) / a computer / you / Can / use /

_____? _____.

2 Write sentences about things you *can* and *can't* do.

Example: *I can't speak Japanese.*

(1) _____.

(2) _____.

(3) _____.

3 Find four more strange things in the picture.

(1) <u>Monkeys can't fly</u>

_____.

(2) _____

_____.

(3) _____

_____.

(4) _____

_____.

(5) _____

_____.

Review

Lesson 10

At the market

1 Complete the sentences.

1 ___There is a lot of___ coffee.

2 _____ water.

3 _____ apples.

4 _____ grapes.

2 Answer the questions.

1 Is there a computer? ___Yes, there is___.

2 Are there any books? _____.

3 Is there any meat? _____.

4 Are there any bananas? _____.

3 Help Eric to find the treasure on the Fun Pages:

a statue	a painting	a ring	a necklace	a crown
a ruby	a bracelet	a medal	pearls	gold

Look for one of the objects on this page! There's _____.

1 Complete the pairs of affirmative and negative sentences.

1 I ride my bicycle every day.

   <u>I don't ride my bicycle every day</u>.

2 My friend can swim very well.

   _____.

3 _____.

   Tom doesn't go to school by bus.

4 _____.

   They weren't studying yesterday afternoon.

5 We're going to have a party on Monday.

   _____.

Points

1 pt. ___

1 pt. ___

1 pt. ___

1 pt. ___

2 Complete the sentences with the comparative or superlative form of the adjective in parentheses.

red book $5   blue book $6   green book $7

1 The blue book is (expensive) _____
   than the red book.

2 The green book is (expensive) _____
   _____.

3 The red book is (cheap) _____
   than the blue book.

4 The red book is (cheap) _____.

1 pt. ___

1 pt. ___

1 pt. ___

1 pt. ___

3 Compare the prices using *as ... as*.

1 The red book isn't _____
   the green book.

2 The green book isn't _____
   the red book.

1 pt. ___

1 pt. ___

Unit 1 Evaluation

Review

4 Read about David and Lisa then write the questions.

David and Lisa are 12 years old. They live in Canada.
David can ride a bicycle but Lisa can't. Lisa has a
computer. David doesn't like tennis.

1 ___Can David ride a bicycle___ ? Yes, he can.

2 _____ ? No, she can't.   1 pt. __

3 _____ ? Yes, they do.   1 pt. __

4 _____ ? No, they aren't.   1 pt. __

5 _____ ? No, he doesn't.   1 pt. __

6 _____ ? Yes, she does.   1 pt. __

5 Write sentences with the words in parentheses.

1 (the president, has to)
   ___The president has to work very hard___.

2 (my friends, don't have to)
   _____.   1 pt. __

3 (the teacher, has to)
   _____.   1 pt. __

6 Make predictions with *will* and *won't*.

In 2020…

1 my town ___will be bigger___.

2 the world _____.   1 pt. __

3 this country _____.   1 pt. __

4 I _____.   1 pt. __

Total   __
20 points

Unit 1 Evaluation

17

Present perfect

Affirmative and negative

1 Complete the sentences with *has* or *hasn't*.

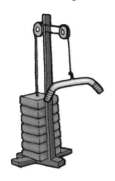

	James	Ben	You
play tennis	✓	x	✓
exercise in the gym	✓	x	x
go swimming	✓	x	✓
pay the bill	x	x	✓
have lunch	✓	✓	x
take a shower	✓	x	✓

1. James ___has___ played tennis.
2. Ben ___hasn't___ gone swimming.
3. Ben ___has___ had lunch.
4. James ___hasn't___ paid the bill.
5. Ben ___hasn't___ taken a shower.
6. James ___has___ exercised in the gym.

2 Write four more sentences about their activities today.

1. ___Ben hasn't gone swimming___.
2. ___James has played tennis___.
3. ___Ben hasn't paid the bill___.
4. ___Ben has a lunch___.

Practice

Lesson 2

Present perfect questions

1 Use the information on page 18 and write questions.

1. _____Has_____ Ben ____gone swimming____?
   No, he hasn't.

2. ____Has____ James ____taken a shower____?
   Yes, he has.

3. ____Have____ Ben and James ____had lunch____?
   Yes, they have.

4. ____Have____ Ben and James ____paid the bill____?
   No, they haven't.

2 Write sentences about your activities at the sports center.

1. I have ____played____.
2. I haven't ____exercised in the gym____.
3. I have ____gone swimming____.
4. I haven't ____had lunch____.

3 Complete the dialogue about your activities.

Interviewer: Have you gone swimming today?

You: ____No, I haven't____.

Interviewer: ____Have you had____ lunch?

You: ____No, I haven't____.

Interviewer: ____Have you taken____ a shower?

You: ____Yes, I have____.

Practice

19

Past simple and present perfect

Complete the past tense and past participle form of the verbs. Write a sentence for each one.

take   I take the bus to school .
__took__   She took her dog for a walk .
__taken__   He's taken a lot of photos .

buy   .
bought   .
_____   .

have   .
had   .
_____   .

drink   .
drank   .
drunk   .

run   .
ran   .
run   .

get   .
got   .
gotten   .

Practice

Lesson 4

| Has she ever...? |
| Have you ever...? |

1 Read the questions and answers about Annie and complete the table.

Has she ever climbed a mountain?   Yes, she has.

Has she ever swum with dolphins?   No, she hasn't.

climbed a mountain		jumped from a plane	x
swum with dolphins		gone whale watching	x
explored the Sahara Desert	✓	gone skiing	✓

2 Write four more questions about Annie and answer them.

1 _____? _____.

2 _____? _____.

3 _____? _____.

4 _____? _____.

3 Answer the questions with *Yes, I have.* **or** *No, I haven't.*

1 Have you ever met a famous person? _____.

2 Have you ever won a competition? _____.

3 Have you ever been to another country? _____.

4 Have you ever swum in the ocean? _____.

Grammar Presentation

I've never...

1 True or False? Look at page 21 and check your answers.

1 Annie has never climbed a mountain.   _____

2 She's never jumped from a plane.   _____

3 She's never explored the Sahara desert.   _____

2 Write two more sentences about things Annie has never done.

1 _____ .

2 _____ .

**3 Write five sentences about yourself with *I've never…*
Use the verbs in parentheses.**
Example: *I've never eaten snails.*

1 (eat) _____ .

2 (drink) _____ .

3 (meet) _____ .

4 (ride) _____ .

5 (go) _____ .

Grammar Presentation

Lesson 6

| I like swimming. |

love   like   don't like   hate

1 Complete the sentences to make them true about you.

1 I _____ watching television.

2 I _____ swimming.

3 I _____ doing homework.

4 I _____ dancing.

2 Write sentences about other activities. Choose from these verbs:

read   ride   watch   eat   play   do

Example: *I like riding my bicycle.*

1 I like _____.

2 I love _____.

3 I don't like _____.

4 I hate _____.

5 _____.

6 _____.

Grammar Presentation

I'm good at cooking.

1 Color the correct box for you.

1 I'm

good at
not good at

cooking.

2 I'm

good at
not good at

drawing.

3 I'm

good at
not good at

singing.

4 I'm

good at
not good at

working with computers.

5 I'm

good at
not good at

running.

2 Write sentences with *I'm good at...* and *I'm not good at...*

1 _____.

2 _____.

3 _____.

4 _____.

5 _____.

6 _____.

Grammar Presentation

Lesson 8

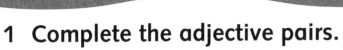

Cooking is fun.

1 Complete the adjective pairs.

fun	boring	interesting	difficult
exciting	easy	expensive	dangerous

_____ fun _____   _____ boring _____

_____   _____

_____   _____

_____   _____

2 Complete the sentences with adjectives from exercise 1.

(1) Climbing mountains is _____.

(2) Learning English is _____.

(3) Cooking is _____.

(4) Going to the movies is _____.

3 Choose activities for these sentences.

(1) _____ exciting.

(2) _____ difficult.

(3) _____ boring.

(4) _____ interesting.

(5) _____ fun.

(6) _____ easy.

Grammar Presentation

Spelling words with *ee* and *ea*

1 Write the words for these pictures.

meat

2 Add the words above to the spelling pattern lists.

Spelling patterns		
words with *ee*		words with *ea*
_____	_____	_____
_____	_____	_____
_____	_____	_____
_____	_____	_____
_____		_____
		_____

3 Add these words to the spelling pattern lists:

| street | leave | week | cheap | sweet |
| feed | see | weak | bean | mean |

Spelling

Lesson 10

Adventures with Eric Explorer

In the Arctic

1 Read the verbs on the pieces of ice. Write the verbs in the –ing form in the correct group.

Group 1 Verbs which double the consonant:

____running____   _____   _____

Group 2 Verbs which take off the last –e:

____riding____   _____   _____

Group 3 Verbs which just add –ing:

____seeing____   _____   _____

2 The last four letters of Eric's favorite activity spell one of the objects on page 15.

It's the _____.

27

1 Write questions with *ever* and the words in parentheses. Complete the answers.

Points

(you, climb, a mountain)

Andy: ___Have you ever climbed a mountain___?

Dan: Yes, ___I have___.

(you, swim, in the ocean)

Andy: _____?   1 pt. __

Dan: No, _____.   1 pt. __

(your sister, go, Canada)

Andy: _____?   1 pt. __

Dan: Yes, _____.   1 pt. __

(she, win, a competition)

Andy: _____?   1 pt. __

Dan: No, _____.   1 pt. __

(your parents, go, to Spain)

Andy: _____?   1 pt. __

Dan: No, _____.   1 pt. __

(they, meet, a famous person)

Andy: _____?   1 pt. __

Dan: Yes, _____.   1 pt. __

Unit 2 Evaluation

2 Read the dialogue again and complete Dan's sentences. Use *never* where it's appropriate.

1 __I've climbed__ a mountain.

2 _____ in the ocean.

3 _____ Canada.

4 _____ a competition.

5 _____ to Spain.

6 _____ a famous person.

3 Complete the sentences.

1 __Playing soccer__ is fun.

2 I'm not good at __swimming__.

3 My friend doesn't like __running__.

4 _____ is dangerous.

5 I'm good at _____.

6 I hate _____.

7 My mother hates _____.

8 _____ is boring.

Points

1 pt. __

1 pt. __

1 pt. __

1 pt. __

1 pt. __

1 pt. __

1 pt. __

1 pt. __

1 pt. __

1 pt. __

Total ___
20 points

Unit 2 Evaluation

If he goes to the Amazon...

1 Match the columns.

If he goes to the Amazon,   he'll explore the rainforest.
If he goes scuba diving,   he'll see beautiful fish.
                                   he'll sleep in a beach hut.
                                   he'll learn to canoe.

He'll sleep. = He will sleep.

2 Write three more sentences about the vacations.

Example: *If he goes to the Amazon, he'll see alligators.*

1. If he goes to Scuba, he'll swim with dolphins.
2. If he goes to the Amazon, he'll sleep in a hammock
3. If he go to scuba, he will visit underwater caves.

Grammar Presentation

Lesson 2

1 Write the words in the correct order.

(1) / he'll / If he / be sick / , / three hamburgers / eats /

If he eats 3 hamburgers, he'll be sick.

(2) / exercise every day / , / get fit / you'll / If you /

If you exercise every day, you'll get fit.

(3) / good grades / If you don't / you won't / get / , / study /

If you don't study, you won't get good grades

(4) / she / , / If they don't / will be angry / help their mother /

If they don't help their mother, she will be angry.

(5) / listen in class / you / If you don't / understand / , / won't /

If you don't listen in class, you won't understand

(6) / , / has / some money / she'll / If she / buy / a CD /

If she has some money, she'll buy a CD.

2 Complete the sentences.

(1) _If they goes swim_ , they'll have a good time.

(2) _If I goes to the shopping,_ I'll be very happy.

(3) _If she doesn't help her sister,_ she'll be very angry.

(4) _If he doesn't come to the party,_ we'll be sad.

Practice

We don't use *can* with *will*. We use *be able to*.
He will *be able to* come tomorrow.

Lucy can't decide what to do this evening.

Should I...

...do my homework?

...go to Karen's party?

...fix my bike?

...paint my bedroom?

Write pairs of sentences with *will* and *won't*.

Example:
If she paints her bedroom, it will look very nice.
If she paints her bedroom, she won't be able to do her homework.

(1) <u>If she goes to Karen's party,</u>_____.

_____.

(2) _____.

_____.

(3) _____.

_____.

Practice

Lesson 4

| If I don't study... |

1 Match the columns.

1 If I don't study for the exam, I

2 If I don't get a good grade, my

3 If my parents are angry, they

4 If they don't buy me a new bike,

won't buy me a new bike.

I won't be able to enter the competition.

won't get a good grade.

parents will be angry.

2 Write a consequence chain with this beginning:

If I go to bed late tonight, _____.

_____.

_____.

_____.

_____.

3 Write a consequence chain with this ending:

_____.

_____.

_____.

_____.

_____, I'll be the happiest person in the world.

may/might **or** going to

pack my suitcase	Monday or Tuesday
buy my ticket	Tuesday
fly to Brazil	Wednesday
look for the treasure	Thursday or Friday
explore the rainforest	Friday or Saturday

1 Read Mrs. Mystery's plans and circle the correct words.

(1) She   is going to / might   buy her ticket on Tuesday.

(2) She   is going to / may   pack her suitcase on Monday.

(3) She   is going to / might   explore the rainforest on Friday.

| may = might |

2 Write sentences about Mrs Mystery's plans with *may/ might* **or** *is going to*.

(1) _She may look for the treasure on Thursday_ .

(2) _____ .

(3) _____ .

(4) _____ .

(5) _____ .

Grammar Presentation

Lesson 6

He may/might go out.

1 Write about your weekend. Use *I might/I may* **and**
I'm going to.

Example: *On Saturday morning, I may go to the mall.*
On Sunday afternoon, I'm going to play tennis.

1 On Saturday morning, _____

_____ .

2 On Saturday afternoon, _____

_____ .

3 On Saturday evening, _____

_____ .

4 On Sunday morning, _____

_____ .

5 On Sunday afternoon, _____

_____ .

6 On Sunday evening, _____

_____ .

2 Make predictions with *may/might.*

1 Next week, _____ .

2 Next month, _____ .

3 In two months' time, _____ .

4 Next year, _____ .

Practice

He could jump into the river.

1 Jack is in danger. Write sentences about how he could escape. Use the verbs in the box.

1 ____He could jump____ into the river.

2 _____ the bridge.

3 _____ the tree.

4 _____ into the jungle.

5 _____ into the jeep.

jump

cross

get

run

climb

2 Complete the dialogue with Jack. Use these verbs:

eat   climb   break   bite   cross   jump

1 You: You ____could jump____ into the river.

2 Jack: The crocodiles ____might eat____ me.

3 You: You _____ the tree.

4 Jack: The snake _____ me.

5 You: You _____ the bridge.

6 Jack: It _____.

Grammar Presentation

Lesson 8

| First conditional with *may/might* |

1 Match the columns.

1 If you get into the jeep, Mrs. Mystery might catch you.

2 If you don't move, the it may not start.

3 If you run into the jungle, panther might attack you.

2 Write three more sentences about Jack.

1 If he <u>crosses the bridge</u> ,_____.

2 If he _____,_____.

3 If he _____,_____.

3 Write a sentence with these words in the correct order.
/ you / If / the rope / hold / be able to / I'll / lift you /

_____

_____

_____.

Spelling words
with silent letters

1 Find the spelling pattern in these words:

might	light	bought	brought	thought	height
night	right	flight	bright	fright	weight

The spelling pattern is _____.

2 Color the letters which are pronounced. Don't color the silent letters.

3 Complete the sentences with –*ght* words.

1 I _____ go to the beach on vacation.

2 I go to bed at ten o'clock at _____.

3 Do you have the _____ answer for this question?

4 What is the _____ of that building?

5 I _____ you were in Canada.

6 What color are these pants? They're _____ blue.

7 I _____ a CD at the mall.

8 He _____ his brother to the party.

Lesson 10

Adventures with Eric Explorer
A puzzle for Eric

Help Eric to guess what Mrs. Mystery has put in the boxes.

1 Read the clues and complete the sentences.

If he opens the blue box, he won't find the treasure.

If he opens the yellow box, he'll scream.

If he opens the brown box, he'll be happy.

The _____ is in the yellow box.

The photo _____.

The treasure _____.

2 Look at the list on page 15. Read the clue and identify the object.

It rhymes with the color of the box.

It's the _____.

1 Write sentences about Dan's plans for the vacation.

Points

> Help my dad at the office ✓
> Visit my grandparents ?
> Learn Japanese ?
> Go swimming once a week ✓
> Get fit ✓
> Make some model airplanes ?
> Give my little sister tennis lessons?

definite plans ✓
possible plans ?

1 He's going to help his dad at the office .

2 He might visit his grandparents .

3 _____ .   1 pt. __

4 _____ .   1 pt. __

5 _____ .   1 pt. __

6 _____ .   1 pt. __

7 _____ .   1 pt. __

2 Write five suggestions for Dan. Use these phrases:

help your mother in the house   go out with your friends
paint your bedroom   study English   teach the dog tricks

1 You could _____ .   1 pt. __

2 _____ .   1 pt. __

3 _____ .   1 pt. __

4 _____ .   1 pt. __

5 _____ .   1 pt. __

Unit 3 Evaluation

3 Put the words in the correct order to make sentences.

Example: *If you get up late, you'll be late for school.*

Points

1 / goes out / Pam / see her friends / If / she'll / , /

_____.

1 pt. __

2 / If / I'll swim / to the beach / go / in the ocean / I / , /

_____.

1 pt. __

4 Write suitable endings for these sentences.

1 If we find the treasure, <u>we will be very rich</u> .

2 If he doesn't come to the party,

_____.

1 pt. __

3 If my sister goes to the park,

_____.

1 pt. __

4 If there are hamburgers for lunch,

_____.

1 pt. __

5 If our teacher gives us a test,

_____.

1 pt. __

5 Write suitable beginnings for these sentences.

1 <u>If he doesn't call his parents</u>, they will be worried.

2 _____,

you will have a good time.

1 pt. __

3 _____,

I might go to the party.

1 pt. __

4 _____,

we won't go to the movies.

1 pt. __

5 _____,

I will be able to help you.

1 pt. __

Total ____

20 points

Unit 3 Evaluation

| The potatoes are washed. |

1 Number the sentences in the correct order.

_____ The French fries are put in a box.

_____ The French fries are given to the customer.

_____ The potatoes are washed.

_____ The French fries are cooked in the oil.

_____ The potatoes are cut.

_____ The French fries are eaten.

__1__ The potatoes are grown in fields.

_____ The oil is heated.

> It *is heated.* = Someone heats it.
> They *are eaten.* = Someone eats them.

2 Underline the verbs in the passive in exercise 1.

Example: *The French fries <u>are put</u> in a box.*

3 Complete the grammar rule.

We make the passive voice with the verb _____
and the past participle.

Grammar Presentation

Lesson 2

Present simple passive

1 Complete the table of past tenses and past participles.

Regular verbs	Past simple	Past participle
pick	picked	picked
blend	_____	_____
add	_____	_____
cook	_____	_____
peel	_____	_____
Irregular verbs		
put	_____	_____
grow	_____	_____
stick	stuck	stuck

2 Complete the sentences with passive forms.

How is tomato ketchup made?

1. The plants are _____ in fields.

2. The tomatoes are _____.

3. The tomatoes _____ peeled.

4. The tomatoes are _____.

5. Flavoring _____ added to the mixture.

6. The mixture is _____.

7. The mixture _____ put in bottles.

8. Labels are _____ on the bottles.

Tomato Ketchup

Practice

Present simple
passive with *by*

1 Read about Zoom computer games and write the names of the countries under the pictures.

Zoom computer games are designed in Australia.
They are made in Japan. They are sold in the United States.

_____   _____   _____

2 Read about how computer games are made and write sentences using the passive.

A computer programmer writes the program.
An artist draws the pictures.
Robots make the games.
Factory workers put the games in boxes.
Drivers take the boxes to the stores.
Customers buy the games.

1 ___The program is written by a computer programmer___ .

2 _____ .

3 _____ .

4 _____ .

5 _____ .

6 _____ .

Grammar Presentation

Lesson 4

| Present simple passive |
| Questions and negatives |

1 Answer the questions with these phrases:

Yes, it is.　No, it isn't.　Yes, they are.　No, they aren't.

1 Are pandas found in Antarctica? _____.

2 Are computer games made in Asia? _____.

3 Is coffee drunk in the United States? _____.

4 Are kangaroos found in Australia? _____.

5 Is English spoken in the United States? _____.

6 Is corn grown in the Sahara Desert? _____.

2 Make sentences with the words in parentheses. Use the negative form of the passive.

1 (pandas, Antartica)

_Pandas aren't found in Antartica_____.

2 (kangaroos, Africa)

_____.

3 (French, Japan)

_____.

4 (corn, Sahara desert)

_____.

5 (coconuts, Alaska)

_____.

6 (polar bears, China)

_____.

Grammar Presentation

A school play

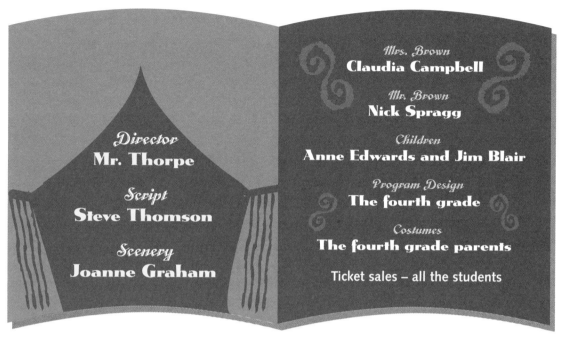

Complete the sentences about the play with the past form of these verbs:

paint   write   play (x3)   sell   design   direct   make

1 Steve Thomson __wrote_____ the play.

2 The fourth grade students _____ the program.

3 Mr. Thorpe _____ the play.

4 Anne Edwards and Jim Blair _____ the children.

5 All the students _____ the tickets.

6 Claudia Campbell _____ Mrs. Brown.

7 The fourth grade parents _____ the costumes.

8 Nick Spragg _____ Mr. Brown.

9 Joanne Graham _____ the scenery.

Vocabulary **P**resentation

Lesson 6

The program was designed by the students.

1 Complete this article from the school newspaper.

SCHOOL NEWS

The fourth grade play was a great success

The scenery ___was painted by Joanne Graham___.

The script ___was written by Steve Thomson___.

The program _____.

The costumes _____.

The play _____.

The tickets _____.

Mrs. Brown _____.

Mr. Brown _____.

The children _____.

Congratulations, everyone!

2 Imagine a play in your school. Write five sentences using these verbs in the passive form:

direct	play	write	make	design

_____.

_____.

_____.

_____.

_____.

Grammar Presentation

It wasn't won by...

1 Read the facts and correct the information in the sentences.

1930 first World Cup soccer tournament; winner - Uruguay

1853 first potato chips eaten

1891 first game of basketball; inventor - James Naismith

1904 first ice cream cone made

1826 first photograph taken

1 The first World Cup soccer tournament was won by Brazil.

It wasn't won by Brazil _____.

It was won by Uruguay _____.

2 The first potato chips were eaten in 1920.

_____.

_____.

3 The first game of basketball was played in 1960.

_____.

_____.

4 Basketball was invented by Magic Johnson.

_____.

_____.

5 The first ice cream cone was made in 1970.

_____.

_____.

6 The first photograph was taken in 1926.

_____.

_____.

Practice

Lesson 8

Who was it written by?

1 **You and your friends have a hit song! Write the name of your song and your band in the Top Ten chart.**

★ **This week's Top Ten** ★

1 _____ by _____

2 Dance all night by The Disco Wonders.

2 **Write the names of your friends in the sentences.**

1 _____ and _____ wrote the song.

2 _____ sang the song.

3 _____ and _____ played the guitars.

4 _____ played the drums.

5 _____ played the keyboards.

3 **Put the words in the correct order. Answer the questions.**

1 / by / the song / sung / Who / was /

_____?

_____.

2 / the guitars / Who / played / were / by /

_____?

_____.

3 / was / Who / written / the song / by /

_____?

_____.

Grammar Presentation

Spelling words with *oo*

1 Underline the spelling pattern in these words:

| foot | food | cook | school | boot | good |

| wood | floor | door | poor | cool | wool |

2 Write six more words with the spelling pattern.

1 z_____

2 b_____

3 l_____

4 r_____

5 t_____

6 m_____

3 Complete the rhyme with words from exercise 1 and exercise 2.

Let's make a snack,
To take to _____.
A monster pizza!
That sounds _____.

Get the ingredients,
And the recipe _____.
Turn on the stove,
Let's start to _____!

Let's go show Mom,
Please open the _____.
Oh, no! The monster pizza
Is all over the _____!

Spelling

Lesson 10

Adventures with Eric Explorer
Tom Lott's treasure

Unit 4

Read the text and make questions with the words in parentheses. Write the answers.

Two hundred years ago, Tom Lott hid some treasure. Two days ago, Eric Explorer's friend, Jack Dawson, discovered the map. Yesterday, Eric found the treasure and took it to the museum. Mrs. Mystery followed him. She wanted the treasure, but it was too late. Eric gave the treasure to the museum. Andrew Atkins, the director of the museum, thanked Eric.

1 (who, treasure, hidden by)

_____Who was the treasure hidden by_____? _Tom Lott_____.

2 (who, map, discovered by)

_____? _____.

3 (who, treasure, found by)

_____? _____.

4 (who, Eric, followed by)

_____? _____.

5 (who, Eric, thanked by)

_____? _____.

Look at Eric's list on page 15. Make one of the objects with the first letter of each last name in the answers.

It's the _____.

Fun Page

1 Write the past simple and past participle of these verbs:

1 go _____went_____ _____gone_____   Points

2 eat _____ _____   1 pt. __

3 take _____ _____   1 pt. __

4 visit _____ _____   1 pt. __

5 drink _____ _____   1 pt. __

6 put _____ _____   1 pt. __

2 Make these sentences passive.

1 Tom painted this picture.

___This picture was painted by Tom_____.

2 My friend wrote this story.

_____.   1 pt. __

3 The children made these models.

_____.   1 pt. __

4 Artists draw the pictures.

_____.   1 pt. __

5 The students write the answers.

_____.   1 pt. __

6 Children buy the games.

_____.   1 pt. __

Unit **4** **E**valuation

3 Make questions from these sentences.

1 The letter was written by Joe.

  Who was the letter written by _____?   Points

2 The stories were written by the students.

  _____?   1 pt. __

3 The boys were stopped by the police officer.

  _____?   1 pt. __

4 The cat was rescued by the firefighter.

  _____?   1 pt. __

5 The classroom was cleaned by Tom and Jason.

  _____?   1 pt. __

6 The cakes were made by Tracy's mother.

  _____?   1 pt. __

4 Complete the sentence sets.

1 This picture was painted by Tom.

  This picture wasn't painted by Tom   .

2 _____.   1 pt. __

  Corn isn't grown in this country.

3 The game was invented by them.

  _____.   1 pt. __

4 _____.   1 pt. __

  The sodas weren't bought by Penny.

5 The exams were written by the teacher.

  _____.   1 pt. __

6 The floor was swept by Joel.

  _____.   1 pt. __

                                        Total ___
                                              20 points

Making questions

Making questions by inverting the order.

be	He is tall.	→	Is he tall?
present perfect (with *has* or *have*)	He has eaten.	→	Has he eaten?
future with *going to*	He is going to go.	→	Is he going to go?

We can add question words.

with *be*	Where is he?
with *present perfect*	What have you eaten today?
with *going to*	When is he going to arrive?

Change these sentences into questions.

He's in the house.
They've watched this video.
They're going to see her on Monday.

Inverted questions

1. _Is he in the house_____?

2. _____?

3. _____?

Wh- questions

4. Where _____?

5. What _____?

6. When _____?

Practice

Lesson 2

Making questions

Questions with *Do, Does* and *Did*

He lives in that house.	➜	Does he live in that house?
They like hamburgers.	➜	Do they like hamburgers?
She talked to him.	➜	Did she talk to him?

We can add question words.

Where does he live?
What do they like?
Where did she go?

Change these sentences into questions.

He wants to go to the party.
They play tennis every Saturday.
She has a new bicycle.
They arrived at six o'clock.

Do/Does/Did questions

1 _____?

2 _____?

3 _____?

4 _____?

Wh- questions

5 Where _____?

6 When _____?

7 What _____?

8 What time _____?

Practice

1 Find the question words and expressions in the chains.

f w h e r e b o w h a t s l w h e n

l r o r i w h i c h k v n e h o w c

x s w h y l p r h o w o f t e n w u

l a z e m d w h a t t i m e q o e r

2 Complete the questions with the words and expressions from exercise 1.

_____ do you play soccer?	At the sports center.
_____ do you play soccer?	On Monday.
_____ do you play soccer?	At 4 o'clock.
_____ do you play soccer?	Once a week.
_____ do you play soccer?	Because I like it.
_____ team do you play for?	My school team.
_____ is the uniform like?	White shorts and blue T-shirts.
_____ do you travel to the games?	By bus.

3 In your notebook write questions about a subject that interests you. Answer them.

Practice

Lesson 4

On vacation

1 Write the vacation words below in the correct categories:

toothbrush   the capital   train   the beach   car   bus
the country   sunbathe   passport   see a show   relax
sunglasses   plane   on a tour   see the sights   hairbrush

things to pack	places to go	things to do	transportation
_____	_____	_____	_____
_____	_____	_____	_____
_____	_____	_____	_____
_____	_____	_____	_____

2 Write questions which you can ask Mrs. Mystery about her vacation.

(1) Which <u>pet are you going to take</u> _____?

(2) How _____?

(3) When _____?

(4) Who _____?

(5) Where _____?

(6) What time _____?

(7) What _____?

Vocabulary Presentation

1 Read the text and match the questions and answers.

Tom talked to Sally. Linda danced with James. David talked to Tracy and he danced with Lucy. Brad talked to Anne and he danced with Amy. Alice danced with John and she talked to Amy.

1 Who did Tom talk to?

2 Who talked to Tom?

3 Who did Linda dance with?

4 Who danced with Linda?

With James.

James did.

Sally did.

To Sally.

2 Answer the questions about the party.

1 Who did David dance with? _____.

2 Who danced with David? _____.

3 Who did Brad talk to? _____.

4 Who talked to Brad? _____.

5 Who did John dance with? _____.

6 Who danced with John? _____.

Grammar Presentation

Lesson 6

Questions with *Who...?*

1 Read the text on page 59. Complete the questions and answer them.

(**1**) Who did Brad _____ with? _____.

(**2**) Who _____ with Brad? _____.

(**3**) Who did David _____ to? _____.

(**4**) Who _____ to David? _____.

2 Write two questions and answers about Amy.

(**1**) Who _____? _____.

(**2**) Who _____? _____ did.

3 Put the words in the correct order to make questions. Answer the questions.

(**1**) / sit / you / Who / do / next to /

_____? _____.

(**2**) / you / Who / next to / sits /

_____? _____ does.

(**3**) / talk to / Who / you / this morning / did /

_____? _____.

(**4**) / called / have / you / Who / this week /

_____? _____.

(**5**) / Who / you / called / has / this week /

_____? _____ has.

Practice

Connectors

1 Complete the sentences with *or, but* or *and*.

1 Tom likes oranges __but__ he doesn't like grapes.

2 Tom doesn't like hamburgers __or__ hot dogs.

3 Sally hates pizza __and__ French fries.

4 Sally likes salads _____ fruit.

5 Lucy doesn't like coffee _____ milk.

6 Lucy likes water _____ she hates sodas.

7 Janet doesn't like hamburgers _____ French fries, _____ she likes pizza _____ hot dogs.

8 Alice likes bananas _____ grapes, _____ she doesn't like oranges.

2 Write sentences about the food you like and don't like. Use the words in parentheses.

1 (and)

_____.

2 (but)

_____.

3 (or)

_____.

4 (and, but)

_____.

5 (and, but, or)

_____.

Grammar Presentation

Lesson 8

1 Match the punctuation with its uses.

(1)	capital letters	at the end of questions
		in answers like *Yes, I do.*
(2)	question marks	to indicate possession
		to indicate surprise
(3)	periods	at the end of sentences
		to indicate contractions
(4)	commas	at the beginning of sentences
		before *but* in long sentences
(5)	exclamation marks	for *I*…
		between words in a list
(6)	apostrophes	for proper nouns

2 Add punctuation and capital letters to these sentences.

(1) what a fantastic car

(2) do you live in the city yes i do

(3) i like maths but its a very difficult subject

(4) thats my sisters notebook

(5) he wasnt working on his computer this afternoon but hes working on it now

(6) does your brother have a car no he doesnt

(7) where do they live in canada

(8) is your friends name richard no its john

Practice

1 Write the words for these pictures.

1 _____

2 _____

3 _____

4 _____

5 _____

6 _____

2 Complete the words with *ou* or *ow*.

1 m_____se

2 t_____n

3 cl_____d

4 n_____

5 l_____d

6 h_____r

7 h_____

8 c_____nt

9 d_____n

10 fl_____er

3 Choose three of the items and draw them in your notebook.

Spelling

1 Read and draw lines to show where the package went.

Who did Mr. Black give the package to?   To the waiter.

Did the waiter give the package to Eric or Mrs. Mystery?   No, he didn't.

Did the waiter give the package to anyone?   Yes, he did.

Who gave the package to Eric?   The police officer did.

Who gave the package to the police officer?   The hotel manager did.

Who did Mrs. Mystery give the package to?   To Mr. Black.

Mr. Black ●   ● Mrs. Mystery

The waiter ●   ● The hotel manager

Eric ●   ● The police officer

2 Answer the questions.

Who had the package at the beginning? _____.

Who had the package at the end? _____.

Look at Eric's list on page 15. Inside the package is something on Eric's list. The letter you drew to join the names is the first letter of the object. It's the _____.

1 Write these sentences with the correct punctuation.

1 Where are you going?

2 do you like hamburgers

3 Jason wants to go home

4 thats great

5 they live in canada

Points

1 pt. __

1 pt. __

1 pt. __

1 pt. __

2 Complete the sentences with these words:

and   but   or

1 I have a bicycle __and__ a skateboard, __but__

I don't have a computer __or__ a CD player.

2 I've been to the United States _____ Canada,

_____ I've never been to Australia.

3 I haven't seen my sister _____ my mother today,

_____ I have seen my brother.

4 They bought some apples _____ some pears,

_____ they didn't buy any oranges.

1 pt. __

1 pt. __

1 pt. __

1 pt. __

1 pt. __

1 pt. __

Unit 5 Evaluation

Review

3 Read the text and complete the questions and answers.

Todd's parents gave him a bike for his birthday. They bought it in a store in the town center. There were two very good bikes there, a red bike and a green bike. Todd chose the green bike because it was faster. Todd rode his new bike on Friday.

1 What __did Todd's parents give him__ ?

    They gave him a bicycle.

2 Where _____ ?

    They bought it in a store in the town center.

3 Which _____ ?

    He chose the green bike.

4 Why _____ ?

    Because it was faster.

5 When _____ ?

    He rode his bike on Friday.

Points

1 pt. __

1 pt. __

1 pt. __

1 pt. __

4 Make two *Who* questions for each of these sentences.

1 Joe gave the box to Amy.

    Who __did Joe give the box to__ ?

    Who __gave the box to Amy__ ?

2 Mel talked to Sarah.

    _____ ?

    _____ ?

1 pt. __

1 pt. __

3 Dawson went to the movies with Alice.

    _____ ?

    _____ ?

1 pt. __

1 pt. __

4 Brad helped Alex with his homework.

    _____ ?

    _____ ?

1 pt. __

1 pt. __

Total ___

20 points

Unit 5 Evaluation

| Prepositions |

1 Choose a preposition for each picture.

up   down   past   off   toward   on top of

past the hill

2 Read the text below and draw a picture of the scene in your notebook.

There are five monkeys and a boat. A monkey is going up a ladder and a monkey is going down a ladder. A monkey is jumping off the boat. A monkey is swimming toward the boat and a monkey is swimming past the boat.

Vocabulary Presentation

Lesson 2

1 Choose a preposition from the list for each picture.

into   through   over   across   out of   under   along

1 _____ the road

2 _____ the house

3 _____ the woods

4 _____ the road

5 _____ the house

6 _____ the bridge

7 _____ the bridge

2 Write the correct preposition.

1 The river goes (into/under) _____ the bridge and the

road goes (over/through) _____ the river.

2 The bridge goes (out of/across) _____ the river.

3 The river goes (through/across) _____ the town.

4 The path goes (along/out of) _____ the river.

5 The path goes (into/over) _____ the woods.

Vocabulary **P**resentation

Follow the directions and complete the sentences.

1 You're at the pier. You want to get to the castle.
Get _____ the boat. Go _____ the lake. Get _____ of the boat. Walk _____ the woods and turn right.

2 You're in the big house. You want to get to the lake.
Walk _____ of the house. Walk along the path to the river.
Walk _____ the river. Walk _____ the bridge.

3 You're at the factory. You want to get to the town. Walk along the path. Walk _____ the bridge. Walk _____ the playground.
Walk _____ the village. Walk _____ the train tracks.

Practice

1 Follow the directions and draw a line to the treasure.

Walk out of the town and over the bridge. Walk past the castle and through the woods. Get into the boat. Go across the lake. Get out of the boat. Walk up the hill. The treasure is under the tree on the hill.

2 Choose a place to hide your treasure on the map. Write directions to find the treasure.

_____

_____

_____

_____

Practice

Reporting orders

1 **Complete what Sam's mother said with these verbs:**

eat   take   be   go

1 She told him to _____be_____ friendly to everybody.

2 She told him to _____take_____ a shower every day.

3 She told him to _____eat_____ healthy food.

4 She told him to _____go_____ to bed early.

2 **Report what Sam's mother said.**

1 Call home once a week.

_____She told him to call home once a week_____.

2 Listen to the camp guide.

_____She told him to listen to the camp guide_____.

3 Take lots of photographs.

_____She told him to take lots of photographs_____.

4 Have a good time.

_____She told him to have a good time_____.

Grammar Presentation

Lesson 6

He told him to...

He told him not to...

1 Put a check next to what Sam's father said.

1 He told him not to lose his ticket.

Lose your ticket. _____

Don't lose your ticket _____✗_____

2 He told him to call them once a week.

Call us once a week. ___✗___

Don't call us once a week. _____

3 He told him not to shout at his sister.

Shout at your sister. _____

Don't shout at your sister. ___✗___

4 He told him not to spend all his money.

Spend all your money. _____

Don't spend all your money. _____✗_____

> When we report orders some words change:
> me → him/her
> your → my/his/her
> us → them

2 Report these negative orders using *He told him...*

1 Don't be mean to your sister.

_____He told him not to be mean to his sister_____.

2 Don't laugh at me.

_____He told him not to laugh at me_____.

3 Don't wait for us.

_____He told him not to wait for us_____.

4 Don't ride your bike in the rain.

_____He told him not to ride him bike in the rain_____.

Grammar Presentation

He asked her to...

He asked her not to...

Report Jack's polite requests.

Help me clean the stone, please.
Follow my instructions, please.
Please don't touch the walls.
Turn on your flashlight, please.
Please take a photo of the stone.
Take the stone, please.
Don't drop the stone, please.
Please read the message on the stone.

① <u>He asked her to help him clean the stone</u>.

② <u>He asked her to follow him instructions</u>.

③ <u>He asked her not to touch the walls</u>.

④ <u>He asked her to turn on her flashlight</u>.

⑤ <u>He asked her to take a photo of the stone</u>.

⑥ <u>He asked her to take the stone</u>.

⑦ <u>He asked her not to drop the stone</u>.

⑧ <u>He asked her to read the message on the stone</u>.

Practice

Lesson 8

Reported orders and polite requests

1 Report what the teacher said to the students.

Be quiet, all of you!

Richard, hand out the books, please.

Sit down, Jennifer!

Don't talk, Matthew!

Do exercise number one, please, all of you.

Clean the board, Jennifer, please.

Jennifer, don't eat in class.

(1) She told them to be quiet _____.

(2) She asked Richard to hand out the books _____.

(3) She asked Jennifer to sit down _____.

(4) She asked matthew not to talk _____.

(5) She asked them to do exercise number _____. one

(6) she asked jennifer to clean the board _____.

(7) she asked jennifer not to eat _____. in class

2 Report four things which people have asked and told you to do this week.

Example: *My mother told me to make my bed.*

(1) My mother told me to do exercise _____

(2) My mother told me to study _____.

(3) My mother told me to lose weight _____

(4) My mother told me to clean _____. my room

1 Write the words in the categories.

scarf	dinner	nurse	short	dirty
word	turkey	star	winter	story
father	thirteen	bird	car	church

ar
scarf
star
car

er
dinner
winter
Father

ir
dirty
bird
thirteen

or
short
word
story

ur
nurse
turkey
church

2 Write the correct vowel + r combination in these words.

b_ir_thday   g_ir_l   nev_er_   numb_er_

th_ir_sty   summ_er_   p_ur_ple   Sat_ur_day

st_or_m   doct_or_

3 Use vowel + r combinations to complete these words.

sh_or_t   sh_ir_t

f_ar_m   f_or_m

p_ar_k   p_or_k

f_ar_   f_or_

b_ur_n   b_or_n

Spelling

Lesson 10

A meeting downtown

1 **Everyone is going downtown. Work out where each person started from and write the number.**

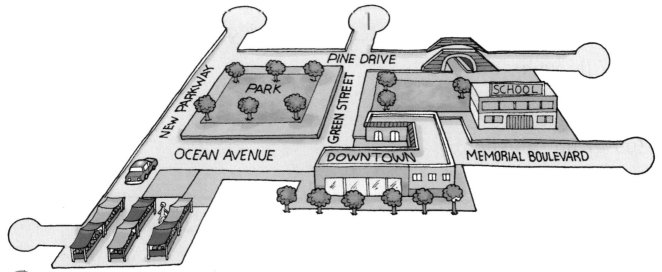

(1) Mrs. Mystery walked along Green Street.

(2) Mr. Black went over the bridge.

(3) Eric went past the school but he didn't go over the bridge.

(4) Annie went past the market and along Ocean Avenue.

(5) Jack went past the park and along Ocean Avenue.

2 **Find five words for types of road on the map.
Choose three of them to complete the table.**

S	T	R	E	E	T	

The letters in the red squares spell one of the objects on Eric's list.
It's the _____.

1 Write the correct preposition.

1 (under / out of / into)

Points

The train track goes ____under____ the bridge.

2 (on / through / off)

I walked _____ the town.

1 pt. __

3 (past / up / through)

He climbed _____ the mountain.

1 pt. __

4 (on / over / toward)

They were running _____ the house.

1 pt. __

5 (out of / on / up)

The road goes _____ the town.

1 pt. __

6 (down / across / into)

The train came _____ the station.

1 pt. __

2 Write sentences with the prepositions in parentheses.

1 (on) ___He is sitting on the chair_____.

2 (past) _____.

1 pt. __

3 (over) _____.

1 pt. __

4 (down) _____.

1 pt. __

5 (across) _____.

1 pt. __

6 (off) _____.

1 pt. __

Unit **6** Evaluation

Review

3 Change these reported requests and orders to direct speech.

1 He told me to be quiet.

   _Be quiet_____!

2 He asked me to give him the book.

   _____.

3 He told me not to leave the house.

   _____!

4 He told me not to watch television.

   _____!

5 He asked me not to open the bag.

   _____.

6 He asked me to help him.

   _____.

4 Report these orders and polite requests with *He asked me...* **or** *He told me...*

1 Open the door, please.

   _He asked me to open the door_____.

2 Polish your shoes!

   _____.

3 Wait for me, please.

   _____.

4 Don't go into the kitchen.

   _____.

5 Don't turn the radio off, please.

   _____.

6 Wash the dishes!

   _____.

Points

1 pt. __

1 pt. __

1 pt. __

1 pt. __

1 pt. __

1 pt. __

1 pt. __

1 pt. __

1 pt. __

1 pt. __

Total   __
20 points

Unit 6 Evaluation

Quotation marks

1 Report this conversation between Annie and Eric. Write what they say in quotation marks.

Eric: I'm going to explore the desert in Peru.

Annie: Can I come with you?

Eric: Of course you can.

Annie: How exciting! It'll be a great adventure.

"I'm going to explore the desert in Peru," said Eric Explorer .

_____ .

_____ .

_____ .

2 Add quotation marks to the second part of the story.

"Here we are," said Eric when they arrived.

It's very beautiful, said Annie. It's the most beautiful place I've ever seen.

We're going to have a great time, said Eric.

But where's our hotel? asked Annie.

We aren't going to stay in a hotel, said Eric. We're going to camp in tents.

But I hate camping! said Annie.

Don't worry, said Eric. We'll have lots of fun.

Grammar Presentation

Lesson 2

Quotation marks

Look at the rules for writing what people say.

Always use quotation marks around the spoken words.
At the end of the spoken words, put an exclamation mark,
a question mark or a comma.

Add speech punctuation to these sentences.

1 "I'm going to the supermarket," he said.

2 "That's a very nice car," she said.

3 "What do you want to do?" I asked.

4 "This is the person who found your book," he said.

5 "Where is the supermarket?" she asked.

6 "Have you ever ridden a camel?" he asked me.

7 "I've never been to the United States," he said.

8 "That's fantastic," they said.

Practice

She said...

I'm a singer.
I like hamburgers.
I don't like hot dogs.
I can sing very well.
I can't draw.

Judy

I'm a student.
I live in Chicago.
I don't like French fries.
I can roller skate.
I can't sing.

Laura

1 Write the name of the person next to the sentences.

(1) She said she was a student. ___Laura___

(2) She said she could sing very well. ___Judy___

(3) She said she liked hamburgers. ___Judy___

(4) She said she didn't like French fries. ___Laura___

(5) She said she couldn't sing. ___Laura___

2 Write sentences about what they said.

(1) (hot dogs) ___Judy said she didn't like hot dogs___.

(2) (Chicago) ___Laura said she lived in Chicago___.

(3) (a singer) ___Judy said she was a singer___.

(4) (roller skate) ___Laura said she could roller skate___.

(5) (draw) ___Judy said she couldn't draw___.

Grammar Presentation

Lesson 4

Reported statements

The chimpanzees are very intelligent.
The snake isn't very friendly.
The mice live in a cage.
The chimpanzees don't live in a cage.
The spider doesn't eat a lot of food.
The dogs can do tricks.

Report what the boy said about the animals.

1 (the chimpanzees)
    <u>He said the chimpanzees were very intelligent</u>.

2 (the snake)
    He said the snake wasn't so very *friend* . *friendly*

3 (the mice)
    He said the mice lived in a cage.

4 (the chimpanzees)
    He said the chimpanzees didn't live in a. cage

5 (the spider)
    He said the spider didn't eat a lot of food

6 (the dogs)
    He said the dog could do tricks.

He said that...

1 Complete the table of reported speech changes.

	changes to...
can	could
live	lived
lives	lived
is	was
are	were
can't	couldn't
don't live	didn't lived
doesn't live	didn't lived
isn't	wasn't
aren't	weren't

We can also use *that* with reported speech.
"I'm very hungry."
He said *that he was* very hungry.

2 Report these sentences with *He said that...*

1. "They can't swim."

   He said that they couldn't swim.

2. "She doesn't like apples."

   He said that she didn't like apples.

3. "The dog isn't friendly."

   He said that the dog wasn't friendly.

4. "It's very cold."

   He said that it's very cold.

Practice

Lesson 6

He said he was an explorer.

My name is Eric.
I'm an explorer.
I'm not a spy.
I live in Canada.
I have a camera.
I don't have a car.
I can speak Spanish.
I can't fly a plane.
Annie and Jack are my friends.

Remember that in reported
statements some words change:
my → his/her
our → their

life
live

Write sentences about the other things that Eric said.

1 (explorer) He said he was an explorer .

2 (Canada) He said he was lived lived in Canada .

3 (a camera) He said he had a camera .

4 (Spanish) He said he could spoke Spanish .

5 (a spy) He said he wasn't a spy .

6 (a car) He said he hadn't a car .

7 (a plane) He said he couldn't fly a plane .

8 (friends) He said that Annie and Jack was his friends .

Practice

83

They said...

I'm going to play with my crocodiles. I'm not going to visit my friends.

I'm not going to leave my house. I'm going to work in my laboratory.

We aren't going to relax. We're going to plan our next trip.

Report what the people said.

Mrs. Mystery

1. _She said she was going to play with her crocodiles_.

2. _She said she wasn't going to visit her friends_.

Mr. Black

3. _He said he wasn't going to leave_.

4. _He said he was going to work in him house in him laboratory_.

Eric and Annie

5. _They said they weren't going to relax_.

6. _They said they were going to plan their next trip_.

Practice

Lesson 8

| He said that he liked his cats. |

I like my cats.
Mrs. Mystery is very strange.
Eric and Annie are my rivals.
I'm going to find the treasure.
I'm the smartest man in the world.
I'm not as strong as Eric.
Mrs. Mystery isn't friendly.
My cats can run very fast.
Mrs. Mystery has very strange pets.
Mrs. Mystery's crocodiles scare my cats.

Mr. Black

Report what Mr. Black said.

1. He said that he liked his cats .

2. He said that Mrs. Mystery was very strange.

3. He said that Eric and Ana were him rivals.

4. He said that he was going to find the treasure.

5. He said that he was the smartest in the world.

6. He said that he wasn't as strong as Eric.

7. He said that Mrs. Mystery wasn't friendly.

8. He said that him cats can't run very fast.

9. He said that Mrs. Mystery had very strange pets.

10. He said that Mrs. Mystery's crocodiles scare him cats.

Practice

1 Underline the vowel combinations in these words:

words with *ai*

| said complain rain explain mail wait waiter |

words with *au*

| laugh August automobile fault saucer |

words with *ea*

| please easy east teacher dream near weather |

words with *oa*

| boat toast coat goal coach soap |

2 Complete the rhyme with vowel combinations.

I have friends all over the world,
N____r, far, here and there,
How is that? I'll expl____n to you.
I have penpals everywhere!

We l____gh, we have fun together,
I don't care if it r____ns all day,
I write to my friends, they write to me
And we always have lots to say!

I write to my penpals every day,
In the North, South, ____st and West,
It's ____sy and fun, that's why I say,
My penpal friends are the best!

Dear Penpal,

A. Friend
2819 Park St.
Townsville, VA
23451

Spelling

Clues

I pack my red bag in the evening.

I help my American friends.

I write a short story every evening.

I listen to loud music.

I eat in an expensive restaurant every day.

I meet my pretty girlfriend at lunchtime.

Change the clues to reported speech.

1. _He said he packed his red bag in the evening_.

2. _He said he helped my American friends_.

3. _He said he wrote a short short story every evening_.

4. _He said he listened to loud music thing_.

5. _He said he ate in an expensive res-taurant_.

6. _He said he met my pretty girlfriend at lunchtime_.

The third letter of the reported verbs tells you where the treasure is

hidden. It's in the _loset_. closet

Look at Eric's list on page 15.

Rearrange the first letters of the adjectives to discover what Eric is

looking for. It's the _____.

1 Add punctuation to this text.

Points

"I don't live in the United States," David said. "I live in Australia."
That's incredible I live in Australia too said Amy
What part of Australia do you live in asked David
In Sydney said Amy

5 pts. __

2 Report the following sentences using *He said*...

1 It's a very nice hotel.

  <u>He said it was a very nice hotel</u>.

2 I can't swim.

  _____.

1 pt. __

3 My sister has two dogs.

  _____.

1 pt. __

4 My parents don't live in this town.

  _____.

1 pt. __

5 I can play soccer very well.

  _____.

1 pt. __

6 My brother is nineteen years old.

  _____.

1 pt. __

Unit **7** **E**valuation

Review
Grammar

3 Write what the people said.

Points

1   He said he was American.

   _I'm American_____.

2   She said her sister couldn't swim.

   _____.   1 pt. __

3   They said they didn't like this town.

   _____.   1 pt. __

4   She said she wasn't very hungry.

   _____.   1 pt. __

5   They said they were going to the stadium.

   _____.   1 pt. __

6   He said he wasn't going to relax.

   _____.   1 pt. __

7   My sister said her friends were playing tennis.

   _____.   1 pt. __

8   My mother said her friend didn't have a car.

   _____.   1 pt. __

9   They said they lived in Canada.

   _____.   1 pt. __

10 He said he couldn't speak Japanese.

   _____.   1 pt. __

11 She said her brother was at home.

   _____.   1 pt. __

Total __

20 points

Occupations

police officer	pilot	secretary
doctor	taxi driver	soccer player	dentist

1 Identify the job.

Do you work in the street? Yes, I do.
Do you wear a uniform? Yes, I do.
Do you have a whistle? Yes, I do.
You're a _____.

2 Write the questions and identify the job.

(a plane) _____? No, I don't.
(in the street) _____? No, I don't.
(a hospital) _____? Yes, I do.
You're a _____.

3 Write three questions for the pilot.

_____? Yes, I do.
_____? No, I don't.
_____? Yes, I do.
You're a pilot.

4 Write three questions for the dentist.

_____? No, I don't.
_____? No, I don't.
_____? No, I don't.
You're a dentist.

Vocabulary **P**resentation

Lesson 2

1 Read the reported questions and answers. Identify the job.

I asked her if she was a police officer. She said she wasn't.
I asked her if she wore a uniform. She said she didn't.
I asked her if she used a machine. She said she did.
I asked her if she worked in an office. She said she did.

She's a _____.

2 Complete the reported interview with the soccer player.

I asked him _____ in an office.

He said he _____.

I asked him _____ a police officer.

He said he _____.

I asked him _____ a uniform.

He said he _____.

I asked him _____ a soccer player.

He said he _____.

3 Complete the reported interview with the taxi driver.

_____ in an office.

He said he _____.

_____ a uniform.

He said _____.

_____ a doctor.

He said _____.

_____ a taxi driver.

He said _____.

Grammar Presentation

We asked her if...

An interview with a teacher.

Do you like teaching?	Yes, I do.
Are you a good teacher?	Yes, I am.
Do you speak Spanish?	Yes, I do.
Do you have a car?	No, I don't.
Do you walk to school?	Yes, I do.
Are you married?	No, I'm not.
Do you have any pets?	Yes, I have a cat.
Are you happy?	Yes, I am.

Complete the reported questions.

1 We asked the teacher __if she liked teaching_____.

2 We asked her _____.

3 _____.

4 _____.

5 _____.

6 _____.

7 _____.

8 _____.

Practice

Lesson 4

He asked me if...

Report these questions.

1 "Does your friend go to the same school as you?"

He asked me _if my friend went to the same school as me_.

2 "Do your parents speak English?"

He asked me _____.

3 "Is your father a pilot?"

_____.

4 "Do your friends go to the mall on Friday?"

_____.

5 "Does your teacher have a cat?"

_____.

6 "Are there any nice parks in your town?"

_____.

7 "Does your mother like reading?"

_____.

8 "Are your friends good at sports?"

_____.

Practice

Reported questions with *if...*

1 Write the name of your favorite movie star.

_____

Write five questions you could ask him/her.

1 Do _____ ?

2 Do _____ ?

3 Are _____ ?

4 Are _____ ?

5 Can _____ ?

2 Report the questions and his/her answers.

1 I asked him/her if _____ .

He/She said _____ .

2 _____ .

He/She said _____ .

3 _____ .

He/She said _____ .

4 _____ .

He/She said _____ .

5 _____ .

He/She said _____ .

Practice

Lesson 6

| Reported *Wh-* questions |

1 Complete the reported questions with the past form of the verbs.

1 "Where do you live?"

He asked me where I __lived__ .

2 "How old are you?"

He asked me how old I _____ .

3 "What do you have for breakfast?"

He asked me what I _____ for breakfast.

4 "What time do you get up?"

He asked me what time I _____ up.

5 "When do you play volleyball?"

He asked me when I _____ volleyball.

6 "Why are you studying English?"

He asked me why I _____ studying English.

2 Report these questions with *He asked me...*

1 "Where are your notebooks?"

__He asked me where my notebooks were__ .

2 "What do you want for your birthday?"

_____ .

3 "When do your friends go to the gym?"

_____ .

4 "Why is your brother looking unhappy?"

_____ .

5 "How do you travel to school?"

_____ .

1 Complete the interview with Annie Intrepid. Use the words in parentheses.

1 (Why, like, exploring)

<u>Why do you like exploring</u>____?   Because it's exciting.

2 (How many, pets, have)

_____?   I have two cats.

3 (Where, live)

_____?   I live in Canada.

4 (What, do, evening)

_____?   I watch television.

5 (Where, go, next trip)

_____   I'm going to go to

_____?   the Ghobi Desert.

2 Complete Annie's report of the interview.

He asked me why _____ and I said because

_____. He asked me _____

_____ and I said _____. He asked me

_____ and I said _____.

He asked me _____ and I said

_____. He asked me _____

_____ and I said

_____.

Practice

Lesson 8

Read this report of an interview with Neil Rogers. Write the questions and answers.

I asked him where he lived. He said he lived in Los Angeles. I asked him if he was American and he said he was. I asked him if he liked Los Angeles and he said he did. I asked him what the name of his next movie was. He said it was "Adventure Zone". I asked him what his plans for the future were. He said he didn't have any plans.

Where _____?

I _____.

_____?

_____.

_____?

_____.

_____?

_____.

_____?

_____.

Practice

sk	sky	desk	skip
sh	shark	fish	shell
sm	small	smile	smart
sn	snail	snake	snow
st	story	study	first
sp	spell	spoon	spend
sw	sweep	swim	switch

Complete the rhyme with the s + consonant combinations.

I can see fi___ ___imming in the ocean,

There's a ___ark going right past me!

I can see birds flying up high in the ___y,

And a ___ake hiding there in the tree!

Do you think I'm walking in the jungle?

Or I'm a diver? No, that's not true,

I'm sitting at my de____ with a pen in my hand,

And I'm writing this ____ory for you!

Spelling

1 Read about the conversation and identify who *She* is.

I asked her…
what her favorite food was. She said it was mayonnaise.
what her favorite color was. She said it was yellow.
what her favorite animals were. She said they were snakes.
Clue: The first letters of her favorite things are the first three letters
    of her name.

She's _____.

2 Identify the person.

My favorite meal is breakfast.
My favorite color is lilac.
My favorite continent is America.
My name is _____.

3 Write a set of favorite things for Eric.

_____.

_____.

_____.

4 Write Mr. Black's favorite things in the shapes.

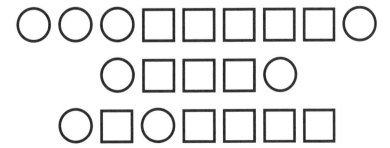

Look at Eric's list on page 15. Use the letters in circles to spell one of the objects.

It's the _____.

1 Report the questions and answers.

1 Where do you live?

I live in Canada.

_I asked him where he lived_____.

_He said he lived in Canada_____.

2 Where does your sister live?

She lives in Japan.

_____.   1 pt. ___

_____.   1 pt. ___

3 Do you like French fries?

Yes, I do.

_____.   1 pt. ___

_____.   1 pt. ___

4 What time do you get up?

I get up at seven o'clock.

_____.   1 pt. ___

_____.   1 pt. ___

5 What is your father's name?

His name's Tony.

_____.   1 pt. ___

_____.   1 pt. ___

6 Do you go to school by bus?

Yes, I do.

_____.   1 pt. ___

_____.   1 pt. ___

Points

Unit 8 Evaluation

Review

2 Read the paragraph and write the dialogue.

I asked her if she liked her school and she said she did. I asked her how old she was and she said she was thirteen. I asked her if she could speak Japanese and she said she couldn't. I asked her which school she went to and she said she went to the City School. I asked her what time she got home and she said she got home at four o'clock. I asked her what she did in the evening and she told me that she watched television.

Points

1 __Do you like your school__ ?

__Yes, I do__ .

2 _____ ? 1 pt. __

_____ . 1 pt. __

3 _____ ? 1 pt. __

_____ . 1 pt. __

4 _____ ? 1 pt. __

_____ . 1 pt. __

5 _____ ? 1 pt. __

_____ . 1 pt. __

6 _____ ? 1 pt. __

_____ . 1 pt. __

Total ___
20 points

He had cleaned his bedroom.

Mr. and Mrs. Robins were out all day yesterday.
They left Jason a list of things to do.

Things to do

Clean your bedroom ✔   Walk the dog ✔

Wash the dishes ✘   Water the plants ✘

Clean the windows ✘   Brush the cat ✔

Take out the trash ✔   Feed the goldfish ✘

1 Look at Jason's list and circle the correct option in the sentences below.

When Mr. and Mrs. Robins came home at seven o'clock…

(1) …Jason (had cleaned) / hadn't cleaned his bedroom.

(2) …he had washed / hadn't washed the dishes.

(3) …he had cleaned / hadn't cleaned the windows.

(4) …he had taken out / hadn't taken out the trash.

2 Write four more sentences about what Jason had and hadn't done when his parents came home yesterday.

(1) _____.

(2) _____.

(3) _____.

(4) _____.

Grammar Presentation

Lesson 2

He hadn't cleaned
his bedroom.

1 Put checks (✔) next to the things Kevin did.

When Kevin got home at 3 o'clock he did his homework until
7 o'clock. He had dinner at 7 o'clock and then he called Sally.
At ten o'clock he packed his school bag and went to bed.

Do my homework ✔   Help my mom in the house
Clean my bedroom   Pack my bag for tomorrow
Have dinner   Polish my shoes
Call Grandma   Tidy my desk
Call Sally

2 Write sentences about what Kevin had and hadn't done when he went to bed.

1. He had done his homework .

2. He hadn't cleaned his bedroom .

3. _____ .

4. _____ .

5. _____ .

6. _____ .

7. _____ .

8. _____ .

Practice

Past perfect with *already*

Combine the sentences.

1 The movie started at six o'clock. They arrived at the movie theater at six fifteen.

  <u>When they arrived at the movie theater, the movie</u>
  <u>had already started</u>.

2 The plane left at ten o'clock. Tom found his ticket at ten past ten.

  _____

  _____.

3 My favorite television program started at five o'clock. I turned on the television at five fifteen.

  _____

  _____.

4 The children went to bed at half past nine. Their father arrived home at ten o'clock.

  _____

  _____.

5 Sally's friend went out at three o'clock. Sally called her friend at twenty past three.

  _____

  _____.

Grammar Presentation

Lesson 4

Past perfect with *already*

1 Complete the sentences in the past perfect using the words in parentheses.

1 When Suzy got up in the morning,
(brother, eat, breakfast)
<u>her brother had already eaten breakfast</u>.

2 When the teacher walked into the classroom,
(students, clean, board)

_____.

3 When I arrived home in the evening,
(father, cook, dinner)

_____.

4 When Jennifer walked into the classroom,
(class, start)

_____.

2 Complete the sentences with verbs in the past perfect.

1 When we arrived at the zoo,

_____.

2 When I arrived at the party,

_____.

3 When the police officer arrived,

_____.

Practice

| Past perfect with *never* and *before* |

1 Write past perfect sentences with *never* and *before*.

(1) In June, Ben rode a camel for the first time.

_____He had never ridden a camel before_____.

(2) In July, Ben and Julie crossed the Sahara Desert for the first time.

_____.

(3) In September, Ben jumped from an airplane for the first time.

_____.

(4) In October, Ben and Julie went to Egypt for the first time.

_____.

(5) In November, Ben climbed Mount Fuji for the first time.

_____.

(6) In December, Julie went up the Eiffel tower for the first time.

_____.

2 Complete the sentences about your own experiences.

(1) Last year I _____ for the first time.

I had never _____ before.

(2) Last month I _____ for the first time.

I had never _____ before.

Grammar **P**resentation

Lesson 6

You should study in the evening.

1 **Put a check (✔) next to the good advice and a cross (✗) next to the bad advice.**

1 I want to get a good grade in the exam.

Study in the evening. _____

Watch television in the evening. _____

2 I want to get fit.

Do some exercise every day. _____

Eat junk food every day. _____

3 I'm always late for school.

Miss the first lesson. _____

Go to bed earlier. _____

2 **Write sentences with the advice from exercise 1. Use** *should* **and** *shouldn't.*

1 _You should study in the evening_____._

2 _____.

3 _____.

4 _____.

5 _____.

6 _____.

Grammar Presentation

should **and** shouldn't

1 Complete the set of movie theater rules with *should* **or** *shouldn't.*

(1) You _____ use your cellular phone.

(2) You _____ talk to your friends.

(3) You _____ arrive late.

(4) You _____ arrive before the movie starts.

(5) You _____ wear a big hat.

(6) You _____ throw your trash in the trash can.

2 Write advice for this boy.
Use *should* **or** *shouldn't* **and these words:**

ride	wear	listen	fast	slowly
busy road		helmet	music	quiet road

I bought a new bicycle yesterday. I'm going to ride it downtown now.

(1) _____.

(2) _____.

(3) _____.

(4) _____.

(5) _____.

(6) _____.

Practice

Lesson 8

should and shouldn't

Give advice to these people. Use *should* and *shouldn't*.

1 I'm eleven years old. I want a pet. I like dogs best but my mother says our apartment is too small for a dog.

_____

_____

2 It's my mom's birthday. She likes music. What gift should I get her?

_____

_____

3 I'm eleven years old. I'm going to take an English exam next week.

_____

_____

4 I'm ten years old. I have a lot of arguments with my little brother. He's seven years old.

_____

_____

5 I'm eleven years old. I get very bored in the school vacations.

_____

_____

Practice

ph or *f* or *gh*?
fish   elephant   fantastic   enough   rough   photograph   laugh

wh or *w*?
white   whistle   watch   want   witch

Read the clues and complete the crossword.

Across
1 They live in the ocean.
2 You tell the time with this.
3 You do this when you hear something funny.
4 A large gray animal.

Down
1 Very, very good.
2 You can make a noise with this.
5 You take this with a camera.
6 A color.

Spelling

1 Complete the sentences about the puzzle.

1 No one (answer) ___had solved___ the puzzle before.

2 Lots of people (try) _____ to solve the puzzle.

3 Everyone (fail) _____ to solve the puzzle.

4 Eric (never, visit) _____ this place before.

2 Look at Eric's list on page 15. Write the letters for each clue and find one of the objects on the list.

The first is in *good* but it isn't in *wood*, ____
The second is in *one* and *through*, ____
The third is in *late* but it isn't in *ate*, ____
The last is in *date* and *do*. ____
It's the _____.

Fun Page

1 **Write sentences about what the children had done and hadn't done when their mother came home at 8 o'clock.**

> At six o'clock Susan cleaned her room and Toby watched television. At seven o'clock Toby did his homework and Susan washed the windows. At seven thirty Toby and Susan cooked dinner.

Points

1 (Toby, his homework)
  <u>Toby had done his homework</u>   .

2 (Susan, her homework)
  _____. 1 pt. __

3 (Susan, the windows)
  _____. 1 pt. __

4 (Susan and Toby, dinner)
  _____. 1 pt. __

5 (Susan and Toby, the dishes)
  _____. 1 pt. __

6 (Toby, his room)
  _____. 1 pt. __

2 **Read the text and write sentences with** *had never* **and** *before.*

> On Saturday Michael went to the beach for the first time. He swam in the ocean. He went on a boat and he water-skied. He built a sandcastle and he looked for shells.

1 <u>He had never been to the beach before</u>   .

2 _____. 1 pt. __

3 _____. 1 pt. __

4 _____. 1 pt. __

5 _____. 1 pt. __

6 _____. 1 pt. __

Unit 9 Evaluation

Review

3 Write advice for these people with *should* and *shouldn't*.

1 I want to have a vacation, but I don't have a lot of money.

Points

You should <u>visit all the nice places near your town</u>.

You shouldn't <u>stay in an expensive hotel</u>.

2 I want to get fit.

_____.   1 pt. ___

_____.   1 pt. ___

3 I sometimes get angry with my friends.

_____.   1 pt. ___

_____.   1 pt. ___

4 I'm always tired in the morning.

_____.   1 pt. ___

_____.   1 pt. ___

5 I have a headache.

_____.   1 pt. ___

_____.   1 pt. ___

6 I have to get a birthday present for my sister.

_____.   1 pt. ___

_____.   1 pt. ___

Total ___
20 points

Unit 9 Evaluation

a lot of/lots

a few/a little

1 Complete the sentences with these phrases:

There is   There are   There isn't   There aren't

1 _____ a lot of traffic in Megatown.

2 _____ a little pollution in Peaceville.

3 _____ lots of noise in Peaceville.

4 _____ a lot of cars in Megatown.

5 _____ a few cars in Peaceville.

6 _____ a lot of trees in Megatown.

2 Write sentences with the words in parentheses and these words:

there is (x 2)   there are   a lot of/lots of   a little   a few

1 (trash, Peaceville)

_____.

2 (people, Megatown)

_____.

3 (pollution, Megatown)

_____.

Grammar Presentation

Lesson 2

How much...?

How many...?

Peaceville

1 Complete the questions about Megatown with *How much* or *How many* and write the answers.

1 ___How much___ pollution is there? ___There's a lot___.

2 _____ people are there? _____.

3 _____ trash is there?   _____.

4 _____ cars are there?   _____.

2 Write questions and answers about Peaceville. Use the words in parentheses.

1 (noise)

_____? _____.

2 (traffic)

_____? _____.

3 (trees)

_____? _____.

Practice

| Quantifiers |

1 Complete the table with these words:

a few   a little   a lot of/lots of

My neighborhood has...

_____ traffic.

_____ people.

_____ pollution.

_____ trash.

_____ stores.

_____ restaurants.

_____ trees.

_____ parks.

_____ noise.

2 Use the information in exercise 1 to write a paragraph about your neighborhood.

In my neighborhood _____

_____

_____

_____

_____

_____

_____

 Practice

Lesson 4

It was so hot that...

1 Combine the sentences with *so*.

1 The movie was boring. I went to sleep.

_The movie was so boring that I went to sleep_____.

2 The exam was difficult. My friend couldn't do it.

_____.

3 The car was very expensive. I couldn't buy it.

_____.

4 The bag was very heavy. He dropped it.

_____.

5 My bed was very uncomfortable. I couldn't sleep.

_____.

2 Write beginnings for these sentences with *so* + adjective.

1 _____ that we watched it twice.

2 _____ that I went to bed at 8 o'clock.

3 _____ that she drank all the water.

4 _____ that he ate it all.

5 _____ that they put on sweaters.

6 _____ that I read it in one day.

7 _____ that she couldn't drink it.

8 _____ that we couldn't eat it all.

Grammar Presentation

Verb table

Complete the verb table.

simple form	present simple	past simple
go	go/goes	went
eat	eat/eats	_____
buy	_____	_____
_____	draw/draws	_____
be	_____	_____
have	_____	_____
_____	_____	_____
_____	_____	_____
run	_____	_____
swim	_____	_____
_____	walk/walks	_____
open	_____	_____
_____	_____	put
_____	_____	_____
say	_____	_____

Practice

Lesson 6

Verb table

present perfect	past perfect	present participle
has/have gone	had gone	going
_____	had eaten	eating
_____	had bought	_____
_____	_____	_____
_____	_____	_____
_____	_____	seeing
has/have closed	_____	_____
_____	_____	_____
_____	_____	_____
_____	_____	_____
_____	_____	_____
_____	had taken	_____
_____	_____	saying

Practice

1 Complete the dialogue with the correct tense of the verb *drink***.**

A: How many glasses of water _____ a day?

B: I _____ about three.

A: _____ you _____ water now?

B: No, I'm not.

A: What _____ you _____?

B: I _____ a soda.

A: _____ you _____ a lot of soda?

B: Yes, I do.

Underline the present simple sentences red.
Underline the present progressive sentences yellow.

2 Complete the dialogue with *call*, *called* **or** *calling***.**

A: What were you doing when Tom had the accident?

B: I was _____ someone on my cellular phone.

A: Who were you _____?

B: I was _____ my friend.

A: What did you do next?

B: I _____ the emergency services.

A: Did you _____ Tom's parents?

B: Yes, I did.

Underline the past simple sentences green.
Underline the past progressive sentences orange.

Practice

1 Complete the dialogue with the verb *eat* **and the words in parentheses.**

A: (what, you, for lunch)

_____?

B: (I, a hamburger)

_____.

A: (how many, you, this week)

_____?

B: (I, five)

_____.

A: (you, a salad with your hamburger)

_____?

B: No, I didn't.

A: (you, a salad, this week)

_____.

B: No, I haven't.

Underline the past simple sentences green.
Underline the present perfect sentences pink.

2 Read and complete the sentences.

1 Last month I went to the beach for the first time.

I _____ never _____ to the beach before.

2 Last year, Amy won a competition for the first time.

She _____ never _____ a competition before.

Underline the past simple sentences blue.
Underline the past perfect sentences purple.

Practice

**Spelling words
that end with** *–tion*

station   condition   nation   addition
subtraction   destination   direction

1 Make *–tion* words from these verbs.

1 imagine _____

2 invite _____

3 collect _____

4 act _____

5 reflect _____

6 decorate _____

2 Complete the rhyme with words that end in *-tion.*

Here's your _____,

To a mystery tour with me,

We'll meet at the railroad _____,

And the best thing is… it's free!

I don't know our _____,

There are so many places to visit,

But if we use our _____,

We can be anywhere in a minute!

1 Eric is writing a book about his adventures. Circle the correct words in the notes and identify the people.

1 We had a lot of / a little adventures together.

   Annie Intrepid

2 She doesn't like camp / camping.

_____

3 She has a / a few crocodiles.

_____

4 He always wear / wears black clothes.

_____

5 Her crocodiles are so / too fierce that I'm scared of them.

_____

6 If I ask her to marry me, I think she accepts / will accept.

_____

7 Mr. Black was / were given the statue by her.

_____

2 Follow the instructions to find the last object on Eric's list.

1 How many letters are there in Annie's full name?

_____

2 How many letters are there in that number?

_____

That's the number of letters in the last object!

It's the _____.

1 Circle the correct words.

Points

1 There is (a lot of) / a few noise.

2 There are a few / a little trees.

1 pt. __

3 There is much / lots of trash.

1 pt. __

4 There isn't / aren't a lot of pollution.

1 pt. __

5 There are / aren't a few cars.

1 pt. __

2 Read the sentences. Complete the questions and answers.

There are a lot of cookies. There is a lot of butter.

There isn't any milk. There isn't any coffee.

1 _How much_ coffee _is there_____?

_There isn't any_____.

2 _____ cookies _____?

1pt. __

_____.

1 pt. __

3 _____ milk _____?

1 pt. __

_____.

1 pt. __

4 _____ butter _____?

1pt. __

_____.

1 pt. __

Unit **10** Evaluation

Review
Grammar

3 Complete the sentences.

1 It was so cold that _____

_____.

1 pt. ___

2 _____

we were late for school.

1 pt. ___

3 My brother was so tired that _____

_____.

1 pt. ___

4 The food was so delicious that _____

_____.

1 pt. ___

5 _____

I bought it.

1 pt. ___

4 Write an example for each of these tenses.

1 Present simple: *I work in an office.*
   (go) She _____.

1 pt. ___

2 Present progressive: *He is walking to the store.*
   (play) I _____.

1 pt. ___

3 Future with *going to*: *We are going to watch a video.*
   (clean) He _____.

1 pt. ___

4 Present perfect: *He has eaten lunch.*
   (open) You _____.

1 pt. ___

5 Past progressive: *They were drinking sodas.*
   (run) She _____.

1 pt. ___

Total ___
20 points

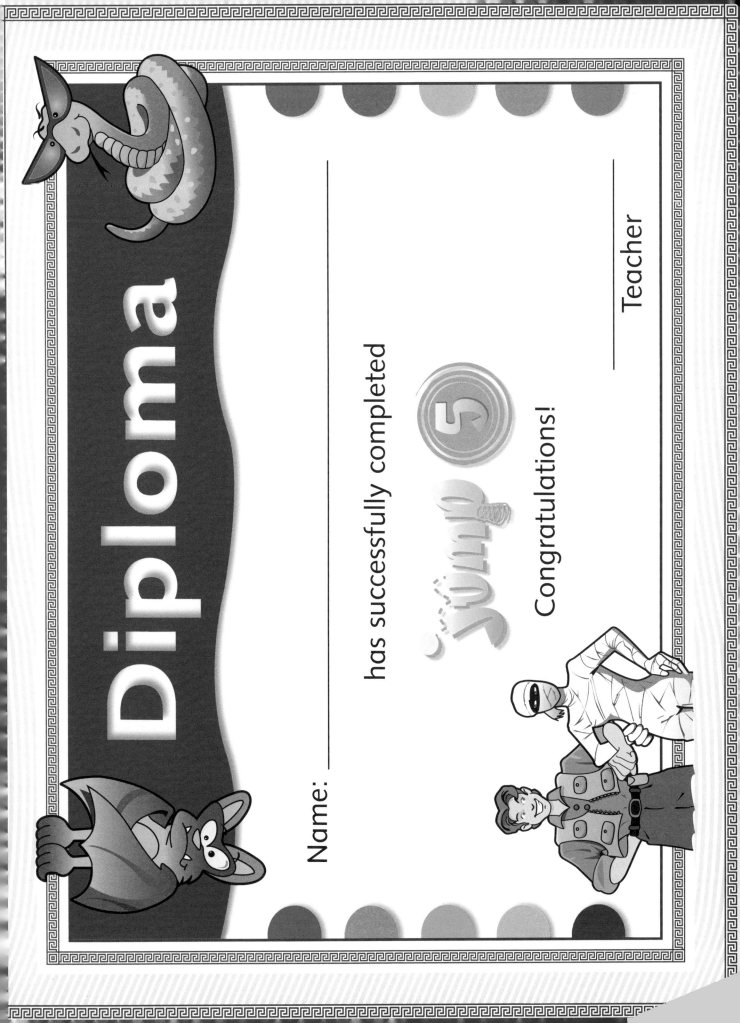

Diploma

Name: _____

has successfully completed

Jump 5

Congratulations!

_____
Teacher